FAMOUS FAMILIES™

OZZY OSBOURNE
AND
KELLY OSBOURNE

LINDA SAUCERMAN

The Rosen Publishing Group, Inc., New York

To my husband, Matt, and to Jack Black, whose performance in the movie School of Rock *was an inspiration for this book*

Published in 2005 by The Rosen Publishing Group, Inc.
29 East 21st Street, New York, NY 10010

First Edition

Library of Congress Cataloging-in-Publication Data

Saucerman, Linda.
Ozzy and Kelly Osbourne / Linda Saucerman. — 1st ed.
    p. cm. — (Famous families)
Includes bibliographical references and index.
Discography: p.
ISBN 1-4042-0262-5 (library binding)
1. Osbourne, Ozzy, 1948—Juvenile literature. 2. Osbourne, Kelly, 1984—Juvenile literature. 3. Rock musicians—England—Biography—Juvenile literature.
I. Title. II. Series.
ML3930.O82S28 2005
782.42166'092'2—dc22

2004012434

Manufactured in the United States of America

Contents

A LIFE IN ROCK 'N' ROLL

It was a crisp day on December 8, 2003, when Ozzy Osbourne, the fifty-five-year-old heavy metal rocker and star of the MTV show *The Osbournes*, decided to take his four-wheel all-terrain vehicle (ATV) out for a spin on his 150-acre (60.7-hectare) estate in Buckinghamshire, England. Just a few days before, he and his nineteen-year-old daughter, Kelly, had zoomed around the sprawling grounds on their ATVs. It was a great way for the famous father and daughter to relieve stress and have fun before they were to appear live on English television singing a duet of the song "Changes."

But Ozzy's ride on his ATV on this day would almost turn deadly. An MTV film crew was on hand as Ozzy drove along the uneven landscape, going almost 30 miles (48.3 kilometers) per hour. However, what the crew did not capture on film was the frightening moment when Ozzy lost control of the ATV. The vehicle flipped over, tossing and turning with Ozzy unable to

Ozzy and Kelly Osbourne, the famous father and daughter musicians and TV stars, share a happy moment at the 2004 Covenant House California Youth Awards. The Covenant House, a national organization that helps young people with problems such as homelessness and drug abuse, honored Sharon Osbourne, Kelly's mom, for her dedication to helping kids.

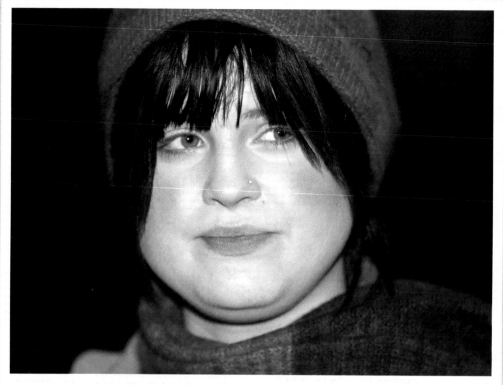

In winter 2003, Ozzy was badly hurt in an ATV accident at the family's vacation home in England. Kelly, who was also in England while the rest of the family was home in California, gracefully handled the flood of questions and attention from the press while nursing her father back to health.

break free. The ATV landed on top of Ozzy, fracturing his collarbone, one vertebra in his neck, and eight ribs, and partially collapsing one of his lungs. When Ozzy's bodyguard reached him, Ozzy was not breathing and his heart seemed to have stopped. The bodyguard had to administer mouth-to-mouth resuscitation—twice—before Ozzy could be driven back to his mansion and taken to the hospital.

During all of this, another MTV film crew was following Kelly around as she promoted her new single, "Changes," a duet with her father. The camera crew was there when she received a phone call telling her of the accident. Kelly instantly began sobbing and ran from the room, leaving the MTV cameraman puzzled as to what the phone call was about. She was immediately driven to the hospital to see her dad. Kelly was the only member of the family in England at the time; her mother and her two siblings were at home in California.

In a later interview, Kelly recounted the scene with her father at the hospital. "And all he kept saying is, 'I love you. I'm going to be OK,'" Kelly told ABC News. "And I'm like, oh my God, my dad's going to die. And I'm all by myself. And it was the horriblest thing that's ever happened to me."

Ozzy later fell into an eight-day coma and remained in the hospital for three weeks. During that time, Kelly took on the role of talking with the media and caring for her famous father. "He's been complaining about the nurses, so we know he's OK. He gave me the thumbs up and stuck his tongue out at me," she said.

Ozzy was going to be all right.

CHAPTER 1

THE PRINCE OF DARKNESS IS BORN

John Michael "Ozzy" Osbourne was born on December 3, 1948, in a small two-bedroom home in Birmingham, England. He was the fourth of six children, and his family was considered working-class poor. That meant that his parents both worked long, hard hours in factories, but they never had enough money. The family didn't have a car and never went on vacation. They didn't even have a proper bathroom in the house and instead used a bucket.

The difference between Ozzy's childhood life and his life now is dramatic. For instance, the Osbournes' mansion in California has three bathrooms, with one being nearly as large as Ozzy's childhood bedroom, which he shared with his three sisters and two brothers. As a child, Ozzy even had to share a mattress, having to squeeze in to fit on one bed with all five of his brothers and sisters.

Along with only having a few shillings (a British term for a few pennies), young Ozzy was bullied and

Ozzy Osbourne on stage with Black Sabbath during the 1970s. His long hair and fringed outfit were a popular alternative look for many of the decade's musicians. Ozzy's howling vocals backed by his band's dark and driving melodies are one of the first examples of heavy metal music.

teased by other kids in the neighborhood. He suffered from dyslexia, a learning disability that made it extremely difficult for him to read or write. This baited the other school kids to call him dumb and laugh at him. (His daughter Kelly also has dyslexia.)

Then, when Ozzy was only eleven years old, two older boys sexually molested him when he was walking home from school. The abuse occurred every day for several months. To make matters worse, one of his sisters was with him once when the boys attacked him and they also threatened her. They told Ozzy and his sister never to tell anyone. If they did, the bullies threatened to kill their mother. Ozzy felt so scared and depressed and had such low self-esteem from the abuse that when he was about fourteen years old, he tried to commit suicide by hanging himself from the clothesline in the family's backyard. Luckily, Ozzy's dad saved him. But neither he nor his sister ever told their family about the bullies and the abuse.

Ozzy Gets Bitten by the Beatles

What also rescued Ozzy was the first time he heard the band the Beatles in 1963. Times were hard for the Osbournes, but one way the family always found comfort was through music. The family would often gather around a small radio and listen to music and sing songs. Most of the music on the radio at that time was classical, swing, or jazz. But what Ozzy heard coming from the radio in 1963 was different. When Ozzy heard the rocking guitars and pounding drums of the Beatles, he instantly became hooked on the raw energy of the music and the idea of becoming a musician. But Ozzy was no different than any other young boy in England at the time. Beatlemania was sweeping across Europe and was about to invade America. Everyone wanted to be like the Beatles.

Because of Ozzy's difficulties in school, he decided not to pursue his dream through formal education and music lessons. Instead, he dropped out of school when he was fifteen. (School is not very popular with the Osbournes. His wife, Sharon, dropped out of school at fifteen, his daughter Kelly quit at sixteen, and their two other children, Aimee and Jack, also do not have their high school diplomas.)

> **Fun Fact**
>
> When Ozzy was a boy, he appeared in a school production of *The Pirates of Penzance*, a popular musical written by the famous British duo William Gilbert and Arthur Sullivan.

After dropping out of school, Ozzy ended up working odd jobs as an errand boy, as a plumber's assistant, and even at the same car factory as his mother. At the factory, he worked in a soundproof room with a conveyor belt that ran through it. On the conveyer belt were car horns, and it was Ozzy's job to set off these horns to test if they worked. For nearly every minute of the eight hours he worked each day, Ozzy heard the blast of a car horn. It was quite depressing and not exactly music to this aspiring singer's ears. But Ozzy's days of blowing horns were numbered. He soon would be blowing away excited fans with his voice, lyrics, and stage antics.

Schoolmates Become Bandmates

When he was eighteen years old, he met a young man who was looking for a singer for his new rock band. Although Ozzy had done most of his singing in the shower and could not play any instruments, he convinced the man that he was right for the job.

Ozzy's dad, who was often not the most loving man to Ozzy and the family, actually helped Ozzy launch his music career. He got a loan from the bank for $300 and used it to buy Ozzy a fifty-watt amp and microphones for Ozzy's first band, the Approach. That band didn't last long, but Ozzy soon hooked up with other guitarists, drummers, and guys from his neighborhood. They created a bunch of other bands that sometimes lasted for just a few days or for several months.

By 1969, Ozzy had been in and out of many bands while still living with his parents. Along the way, he was writing songs, learning about music, and making friends. During this time, he met some local musicians: a guitarist named Tony Iommi, a bassist named Terrance "Geezer" Butler, and drummer Bill Ward. All of them grew up less than a mile from each other, knew each other from school, and had endured pretty rough childhoods. For Ozzy and these three guys, playing music together became a way to forget about all of their problems and release their frustrations.

The Birth of Black Sabbath

Around the time that Ozzy and his bandmates were playing, the world was focused on the war in Vietnam and fighting for civil rights in the United States. Many teenagers and college-age kids were rebelling against society in the 1960s, by protesting, refusing to go to war, and taking drugs, such as LSD, which causes hallucinations. A lot of the music that came out of this era was influenced

Pictured here in 1975, Ozzy (*seated*) poses with the rest of Black Sabbath. All four musicians knew each other from school and began playing music together while they were still in their teens. Before naming the band after a popular Italian horror film, Ozzy and his bandmates called themselves Polka Tulk, and then Earth.

by LSD and the celebration of peace and love. Even Ozzy's beloved Beatles were creating what was being called psychedelic music during these years.

But Ozzy and his new bandmates decided that they wanted to go in a completely opposite direction by scaring people with their music. The four of them loved horror movies, so they named themselves after a popular film called *Black Sabbath*. Adding to the band's creepiness was Iommi's fingers. He cut off the tips of his fingers in an accident while working at a factory, so he made special metal tips to wear on his fingers and loosened the strings on his guitar. The end result was a deep, rumbling-type noise instead of the usual twang of the guitar.

In addition to sounding like satanic misfits, Black Sabbath's members looked the part, too. They would show up for gigs wearing mismatched and ragged clothes, as well as large metal crucifixes (that Ozzy's dad had made) around their necks. Black Sabbath played small clubs where it freaked out and even angered audiences. During one performance, Ozzy poured a can of purple paint over his head and sang stone-faced as the paint dripped down his face. A lot of their concerts ended with the band members getting into fights with people who had come to hear them play. Ozzy wasn't much of a fighter, so as his bandmates threw punches, Ozzy took advantage of the chaotic scene and stole money from the purses of women in the audience.

Sabbath Takes Off

Despite the fact that some people hated Black Sabbath, the band's popularity began to spread. The band soon teamed up with a manager

who got it more gigs and helped it record an album. In the book written by the Osbournes, *Ordinary People*, Ozzy recalls when he brought home his first Black Sabbath album (entitled *Black Sabbath*) and had his mom and dad listen to it. Because of its ominous music and lyrics about death, Ozzy's parents looked tense and his dad wondered aloud if his son was insane.

Fun Fact

Ozzy is so accustomed to being called by his nickname that he no longer responds when someone calls out his real name, which is John.

If Ozzy was insane, he was about to become one incredibly famous crazy man. Black Sabbath began touring all over the United Kingdom and Europe, and through word of mouth, their album reached the top 10 in the United Kingdom. The band's label, Warner Brothers, didn't shy away from the dark overtones of the music. In fact, the record label even boasted about it in a radio advertisement, by describing it as "music as gentle as an open wound." It definitely was not music for the faint of heart. Some of Black Sabbath's most famous songs, such as "Paranoid," "War Pigs," and "Iron Man," were on their second album, *Paranoid*, and influenced not only later bands of the 1970s and 1980s, but continue to inspire new bands, such as Slipknot and Limp Bizkit. Ozzy and Black Sabbath have been credited with creating the music genre now called heavy metal.

The Future Sharon Osbourne

During this time, Black Sabbath hired Don Arden as its manager. Don's daughter, Sharon, worked as a receptionist. She had a smart

> **Fun Fact**
>
> The Osbournes' dog Minnie has the nickname Queen of Metal because she goes everywhere with Sharon Osbourne, the original Matriarch of Metal.

mind for business and soon learned a lot about music and about Ozzy. When Ozzy and Sharon first met in the early 1970s, they were instantly smitten, but Ozzy was engaged to be married to a woman named Thelma Mayfair. Thelma and Ozzy would have a rough marriage, but during it the couple would have two children: Jessica Starshine and Louis. Throughout Ozzy's marriage, though, Sharon would be on the sidelines helping him and Black Sabbath.

In 1979, Ozzy left Black Sabbath and was heavily using drugs and alcohol. Ozzy claims he quit the band, but other members of Sabbath say that they kicked him out. Either way, Ozzy had sunk into a deep depression and was abusing his body. But, luckily, this is when Sharon reentered his life. She saw the greatness in Ozzy and would not sit idly by as he drank himself to death. She pulled him out of his depression, became his manager, and helped him embark on a solo career.

Ozzy Bares His Teeth

But Sharon's efforts to promote Ozzy sometimes backfired because Ozzy was so unpredictable. One particular incident is legendary in the long, strange history of rock 'n' roll.

In May 1981, Sharon and Ozzy were set to meet with top record executives. For the meeting, Sharon purchased three white doves and told Ozzy that he was to release them as he came into the room full of

CBS Records executives. Sharon thought the releasing of the doves would be a fantastic moment that would cause the executives to remember Ozzy when it came time to promote musicians. But what Sharon didn't count on was that Ozzy was extremely drunk at the time. So when he entered the room, he released two of the doves (he kept the third one tucked inside his pocket) and sat down on the lap of a woman who happened to be a publicist—the very same woman who would be in charge of promoting Ozzy and his music. The two doves fluttered nervously around the room and one then landed on Ozzy's lap. Ozzy quickly picked up the bird, bit off its head, and threw the flapping body on the table! A photographer in

By 1986, Ozzy had cut off his hair and his performances included live bats and pig's blood. That same year, he recorded his solo album *Bark at the Moon*, which went platinum (more than 1 million copies sold).

the room took a photo of Ozzy on the woman's lap as he looked into the camera with a face like a madman and blood running down his chin. Sharon and Ozzy soon made a hasty retreat, but not before Ozzy would bite off the head of the third dove and throw it on the receptionist's desk on the way out the door! Sharon started laughing so hard she wet her pants. She was either laughing out of embarrassment or she really did think it was funny—you never can tell with Sharon.

Butcher Boy

One of Ozzy's most disgusting jobs before he became a musician was at a slaughterhouse where he butchered pigs, cows, and other animals. Ozzy would later use this nasty job as inspiration for his *Diary of a Madman* tour in 1981 and 1982. Onstage, Ozzy played with pig guts and blood, and tossed them into the audience. Word spread about the disgusting stage antics, and guests started coming to shows with their own stage props to throw back at Ozzy, including a live bat at a show in Des Moines, Iowa, in 1982. When the bat was tossed up on stage, Ozzy promptly picked it up and bit the head off and spit it out! He would later say that he thought the bat was a rubber toy. Well, he soon learned that biting a live animal is no child's play. Because bats sometimes carry rabies, Ozzy had to go to the hospital and receive several painful shots of medicine. In 2002, Kelly would also bite the head off a bat—albeit one made of chocolate—during a music video for her song "Shut Up."

Bitten by Love

Despite Ozzy's tendency to bite animals, Sharon must have thought Ozzy was crazy in a cute way. In 1982, the couple was married in Maui, Hawaii, less than one year after Ozzy divorced his first wife. Ozzy's dove-biting stunt didn't go exactly as Sharon had hoped, but it did give him a lot of attention—both good and bad—and Sharon was there by his side to help him take advantage of all of the publicity. The success of his albums *Blizzard of Ozz, Diary of a Madman*, and others created thousands of Ozzy devotees who loved banging their heads to songs such as "Crazy Train," "Flying High Again," and "Mr. Crowley."

But headbangers didn't stop rocking out to Ozzy when the 1990s came around. Ozzy kept cranking out hit songs during this decade, such as "Mama, I'm Coming Home" and "No More Tears," and went on tour with popular bands who were much younger than Ozzy, such as Mötley Crüe and Bon Jovi.

Ozzy's love of music and his devotion to Sharon have helped Ozzy not only stay alive, but also become a millionaire and a successful musician who has sold more than 35 million records worldwide.

Ozzfest

In 1995, Sharon wanted Ozzy to be a part of Lollapalooza, a popular concert festival where more than a dozen different artists appeared on the same lineup and toured together throughout the United States. But the organizers of Lollapalooza told her that the forty-seven-year-old Ozzy was "too old."

Offended, Sharon created Ozzfest,

In July 1982, Ozzy married Sharon. Earlier that year, Ozzy's guitar player and close friend, Randy Rhoads, died in a plane crash. Sharon, who is also Ozzy's manager, helped him recover from the shock of his friend's death.

a heavy metal festival with Ozzy as the headline act. In the end, Ozzy and Sharon got the last laugh. Lollapalooza was only successful for a few more years after 1995 before it fizzled away. Meanwhile, Ozzfest continues to rock and sell out venues in every city that it visits. Sharon and Ozzy are definitely a force to be reckoned with, and they make a loving and successful team.

 **CHAPTER 2**

KELLY MAKES SOME NOISE

Growing up in the house of Ozzy and Sharon, the Osbourne children have been exposed to music and the entertainment business their entire lives. Kelly, the middle child, had been on tour with her dad from the time she was very young, riding in tour buses, hanging out in the dressing rooms, and watching from backstage. But on the day of Kelly's fifth birthday, her dad had a surprise for her—he brought her onstage during a show in Japan. "I was terrified because I'd never seen so many people," she says in *Ordinary People*. "They were just looking at me and I was like, 'Ahhh!' All of these people were here to see my dad—and all of them sang along. It was like some secret society I didn't get. I thought every dad did what my dad did."

The Osbournes Opens the Door

On March 5, 2002, *The Osbournes* debuted on MTV. The impact of the show was immediate, and *The*

Kelly shows characteristic Osbourne stage presence while performing her hit song "Shut Up" at the 2003 American Music Awards. Known for her rude lyrics and attitude, Kelly follows in the footsteps of two of her music idols: Debbie Harry of Blondie, and Pat Benatar.

Ozzy, Sharon, Aimee, and Kelly Osbourne gather for a family portrait in 1984. Aimee, the Osbourne's first child, does not appear on *The Osbournes* and, unlike her parents and siblings, does not have her own Osbourne action figure.

Osbournes made entertainment history when it became the highest-rated original program in MTV's twenty-one-year history. The reality TV show was an instant hit as it followed the everyday lives of this eccentric rock 'n' roll family. The show gave the viewer an intimate portrait, showing the Osbournes doing everything from fighting with their neighbors by tossing a cooked ham into their yard to cleaning up after their dogs that weren't properly housebroken.

One of the most striking elements of the show was how much profanity the Osbournes used, not only when they fought with each other but also in their daily conversations. With nearly every word being a swear word on the show, the censors at MTV sometimes had to "bleep" out almost complete sentences. But besides cussing at each other, *The Osbournes* also showed how much this family loves each other. What was really interesting is that many viewers only knew of Ozzy as this crazy man who had bitten the head off of a bat. On *The Osbournes*, they saw that Ozzy also tries to be a good father and a dedicated husband. He definitely isn't as straight and narrow as other classic TV dads, but Ozzy does provide the same love, support, and discipline to his kids.

In one episode, for example, Kelly shows her dad a tattoo of a pink heart that she got on her hip. Ozzy, who is covered in tattoos, scolds Kelly for not consulting with her parents and insists that she tell her mom. Kelly tries to weasel out of telling Sharon, but Ozzy is persistent and eventually Kelly has to own up to what she did.

Language of Love

Sometimes it seems the Osbournes are speaking a different language, using words that only they seem to know. One example is "wobblers," the word that Sharon and the rest of the family use to describe the tantrums that Kelly sometimes throws. These tantrums involve a lot of screaming, huffing, door slamming, and days of Kelly not speaking to whomever has angered her.

Daddy's Little Rock Star

In 2002, just a few months after the first few episodes of *The Osbournes* aired, it became apparent that the public adored Kelly. Knowing that she loves music, Kelly and her family realized that it was the perfect time for her to belt out some songs of her own and see if she could make it as a singer. In 2002, she recorded a punky and poppy version of Madonna's "Papa Don't Preach" and shot a video for it. Fans of *The Osbournes* loved the song and video, making Kelly even more famous.

Then in May 2002, Kelly was asked to perform the song live at the MTV Movie Awards. The huge audience at the theater included

Kelly shows up in hot pink for her performance at the 2003 MTV Movie Awards. At the previous year's awards, Kelly made her debut singing performance with a remake of Madonna's song "Papa Don't Preach," which went straight to the top of the British pop charts.

celebrities Nicole Kidman and Eminem, and millions of people were watching at home. The usually confident Kelly was extremely nervous before the show—it would be her first live performance. But her stage fright was somewhat calmed by Ozzy, who called several times from London to wish her good luck and filled up her dressing room with so many flowers that there was hardly enough room for her clothes and makeup!

Kelly's next musical move was to record an album. Unlike Ozzy's experience with his parents hearing his first album and thinking he was insane, Kelly wasn't worried that her dad would think she was crazy because of her music. (Although Ozzy is constantly saying that his family is nuts!) However, Kelly was nervous about playing her album for her dad. She wanted to make Ozzy proud not only because he is her dad, but because he's also a living rock legend. The listening session between father and daughter was caught on film by *The Osbournes'* crew. Later, TV viewers watched as a nervous Kelly kept glancing at her dad as they sat together on the couch as her CD played. As the song

In 2002, Kelly's debut CD, *Shut Up*, was released. Kelly promoted her music by signing copies of *Shut Up* at various music stores. Here, she poses at the Virgin Megastore in New York City.

"Come Dig Me Out" ended, Ozzy leaned over and gave Kelly a kiss and told his daughter, "You should be really proud of yourself. I know I am."

Later that year, Kelly performed her first full concert in New York City as Ozzy and the rest of her family cheered her on. Then, in September 2003, father and daughter teamed up, as Kelly became the opening act for Ozzy's tour of the United Kingdom.

Fun Fact

In 2003, Kelly refused to shower or bathe for almost a whole month—just call her smelly Kelly!

It was the first time Ozzy and Kelly had ever performed on the same stage.

While on tour with her dad, Kelly performed songs from *Shut Up* and *Changes*, her two albums, which deal with teen issues such as heartache, parents, and just trying to have fun in a crazy world.

Tattoo You

Some of Ozzy's tattoos

(At least the ones we can see. Sharon probably knows of more!)
- Red-hooded Grim Reaper on the left side of his chest
- Blue dragon with red flames on the right side of his chest
- Bat and woman's face on his upper left shoulder
- Rose on his right shoulder, with the word "Sharon"
- Dagger on his right arm
- Unreadable symbols and a number 3 on his right arm
- Demon with flames running down his right arm to his wrist
- The word "Thanks" on his right palm
- Skull with knife on his left arm
- Dagger with "Ozzy" banner on his left arm
- Stick-man figure on his left wrist
- A series of letters on his left palm, starts with "A"
- Letters "O," "Z," "Z," and "Y" on knuckles of his left hand (Ozzy did this one himself while serving a two-month prison sentence in 1965 for burglary)

- Happy faces on his knees (Ozzy said he did these himself to impress some girls he met when he got out of prison)
- Sword on his right thigh

Kelly's tattoos

(Not as scary-looking, but almost as numerous!)
- Pink heart on her hip (her first tattoo)
- Heart on her right pinky finger
- "Jack" on her right wrist
- Lock and key with "Daddy" written above it and a banner that says "This too shall pass" on her left arm
- Star on the back of her neck
- Angel wings on her shoulder blades
- Tinkerbell on her lower back
- Skull and crossbones on her feet

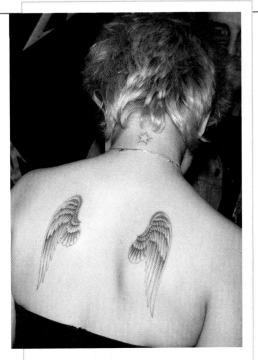

Kelly went with a blonde angelic look for MTV's 2003 mtvICON tribute to the long-lasting heavy metal band Metallica. Honoring Metallica's influence on her generation of musicians, she said, "Bands like Metallica and Mötley Crüe and all that stuff, I've known them since I was a baby."

CHAPTER 3

CHANGES FOR FATHER AND DAUGHTER

A music video opens with a home movie of Ozzy getting a hug from a blond-haired Kelly who looks to be about five years old. The video then shows Kelly all grown up, with her jet-black hair, crimson lips, and porcelain skin. She sits in a chair with a red velvet curtain behind her that is covered with Osbourne family photos. Kelly begins singing "Changes," a song first sung by her dad back in 1972, before Kelly was even born.

When the second verse begins, a different voice is heard and the camera shows another chair, revealing Ozzy. But unlike the original version of "Changes," which is a song about a man and a woman falling out of love, the words Ozzy sings depict another situation—a daughter growing up and a father learning to let go of his little girl. Kelly then

Kelly and Ozzy sang together at London's 2004 Olympic Torch Concert, which was held in the famous London Mall before 70,000 lucky ballot winners. The concert celebrated the arrival of more than 140 torchbearers who carried the Olympic flame through London for the first time since 1948, when England hosted the Olympic Games.

Ozzy and his assistant Tony Dennis, with the ever-present TV crew, after lunching with friends while filming the Hawaiian episode of *The Osbournes*. The fourth and final season of *The Osbournes* aired in the fall of 2004. Each family member is currently pursuing other projects.

sings, "We've shared the years, we've shared each day. I love you daddy, but I've found my way." The video continues cutting back and forth between old home movies and recent footage from *The Osbournes*, conveying the bond between father and daughter that has grown over the years.

Kelly always wanted to record one of her dad's songs, but she never knew which one. She also didn't want to offend the legions of dedicated fans who love her dad's music. Then she listened again to "Changes," from *Black Sabbath Vol. 4*, and after changing the words a bit, realized she had a new special song that would make a beautiful duet—the perfect way to honor her father.

The public realized the song was special, too, making it the number-one song in the United Kingdom for several weeks in December 2003 and January 2004, which was shortly after Ozzy suffered the near-fatal ATV accident on his English estate.

A Knight to the Rescue

No Osbourne collaboration is complete without some fighting. For the duet "Changes," recorded with Kelly in 2003, Ozzy thought that the song needed a choir for backup music. Kelly was strongly against it and argued that the song didn't need the choir. They fought and fought and could not reach an agreement. So they decided to have family friend, rock legend, and honorary knight Sir Elton John make the final decision. Elton listened and ruled that the choir should be added to the song. Thus, another Osbourne crisis came to a happy end. However, the visit with Elton did end on a sour note. During the Osbournes' trip to France to see Elton, Kelly suffered from food poisoning that left her vomiting all night, forcing her to cancel some of the concerts she was to perform with her dad.

CHAPTER 4

A Bad Inheritance

Along with their love of music, Ozzy and Kelly share another family trait—substance abuse. In *Ordinary People*, Ozzy recalls how his father drank beer at the local pub every day after work. Ozzy often had to sit outside the pub and wait and wait until his father had his fill of drink. When he was fourteen years old, a man inside the pub saw Ozzy sitting outside and passed him a beer through the window. This was the first time Ozzy ever drank alcohol. He ended up drinking six beers that day, got drunk, and couldn't find his dad. He woke up the next morning alone and confused in a park near the pub.

But this would not be the last time Ozzy would drink or get high. With the money he earned from odd jobs and then later in Black Sabbath, he would buy drugs and alcohol. The band even wrote a song called "Sweet Leaf," which described how much the band members enjoyed marijuana. But for Ozzy, his drug use became so intense that even his buddies in

Ozzy relaxes at his estate in Buckinghamshire, England. Although he now calls California home, Ozzy still contributes to his native England. He donated money to keep a village shop open near his estate and also to Wexham Park Hospital in Slough, where he was rushed to after his ATV accident.

Jack and Sharon Osbourne sign copies of *Ordinary People: Our Story* at a bookstore in Los Angeles. The Osbournes' book features viewpoints from each family member, including oldest daughter Aimee, who contributed comments on the first season of her family's TV show.

Black Sabbath didn't like being near him. Members of Black Sabbath say that Ozzy became so difficult to deal with during his drug days that he was kicked out of the band.

His drug and alcohol abuse grew even worse until he met up with Sharon and she seemed somewhat successful in helping him stay sober. But Ozzy's accomplishments were short-lived, regardless of Sharon's unwavering support. He would tip back and forth between being totally out of his mind on drugs and booze and then back to small moments of being clean. In fact, Ozzy was at a pub on October 27, 1984, the day his daughter Kelly was born, and he came to the hospital drunk.

But the lowest point came in 1989, when Ozzy came home from Moscow after months of touring with rock bands Bon Jovi, Mötley Crüe, and others. He had been drinking alcohol and doing cocaine for months, and when he got to their home in England, he was in the worst shape Sharon had ever seen him in. A few nights later, Ozzy went insane as a result of large amounts of drugs and alcohol, and tried to strangle Sharon! Luckily, Sharon had installed what she called a "panic button" in case of any emergency. On this night, the emergency wasn't a burglar or a house fire, but her own husband. The police came and arrested Ozzy and even charged him with attempted murder. Ozzy doesn't remember anything he did that night and was shocked the next morning when he heard the police say "attempted murder." Sharon opted not to press criminal charges, but Ozzy did have to enter drug rehabilitation.

Curse of the Osbournes

Many people wonder why Sharon didn't file for divorce immediately after that incident. In fact, she said she did consider leaving Ozzy for good. But she also says that her love for Ozzy and her knowing that deep down he is a good person are what kept her in the marriage.

Today, Ozzy continues to battle with substance abuse but has lately been successful, even giving up cigarettes. Watching Ozzy on *The Osbournes*, and seeing his shaking body and hearing his stammering speech, it is obvious that drugs and alcohol have damaged his body and his mind. It is also obvious that Ozzy is a person who loves his family

Kelly's Colorful Coiffures

In season three of *The Osbournes*, Ozzy told Kelly that he wanted to add green, blue, and other colors to his already red-streaked black hair. Kelly told him it wouldn't look good and added, "You're the Prince of *bleep* Darkness! Not the Prince of *bleep* Lunatics!" But looking back at the hair colors Kelly has had in a two-year time, she is hardly one to give advice!

Kelly's hair colors, 2002 to 2004:

- Light brown/dark blond (her natural color)
- Strawberry blond
- Hot pink
- White blond
- Jet black
- Black with hot pink streaks
- Black with red streaks
- Black with blond streaks
- Black with hot pink bangs (done while she was in drug rehab in April 2004)

dearly, especially Sharon. His love for his wife was especially evident when Sharon was diagnosed with cancer in July 2002. Ozzy was terribly upset by the news and was by her side throughout her illness. After several treatments, her doctors later gave Sharon a clean bill of health, which was a relief to Ozzy and their children.

Ozzy has said on *The Osbournes* that he hoped that his own struggles with alcohol and drugs and his openness about his addictions would serve as an example to his children about the dangers of such substances. Unfortunately, both Kelly and his son Jack have not heeded the warnings. In April 2003, Jack admitted that he was addicted to marijuana and was abusing prescription pills. He was brave enough to ask his family for help and went through a rehabilitation program. Ozzy was saddened by the news of his son's addiction and publicly said that he regrets ever recording the song "Sweet Leaf" and for making drugs seem glamorous. Jack celebrated one year of sobriety in April 2004.

But shortly before Jack's milestone, Ozzy had to come to the aid of Kelly. On the evening of April 2, 2004, Kelly's parents were on the talk show *Larry King Live* and were to discuss the third season of *The Osbournes*, which was to begin airing the following week. Instead, they shared the bad news that Kelly had entered a drug rehabilitation program earlier that day. Earlier, a British photographer had snapped a photo of Kelly buying drugs and then showed the photo to Sharon. Kelly at first denied to her parents that she was using drugs. But after her brother, Jack, found a bag of 500 pills under her bed, she eventually admitted she had a problem.

Kelly arrives at the 2004 pre-Grammy party on her brother Jack's arm. The next night she performed at the Grammy Awards.

"Being a drug addict and an alcoholic myself, I know telling the truth doesn't come easy," Ozzy said. "It's a family illness. It's in the genes."

Kelly did well while in rehab and was reunited with her family a month later. Kelly and her mom celebrated by doing what many moms and daughters do best—they went shopping!

CHAPTER 5

THE FUTURE OF OZZ

Despite Ozzy's ATV accident and Kelly's battle with drugs, these two Osbournes have a lot more to offer their fans.

Ozzfest has been voted the Best Concert of the Year several times by fans, critics, and music magazines. So fans were ready when Ozzy announced shortly after recovering from his accident that there would be an Ozzfest 2004. In fact, in early spring 2004, VIP packages for all twenty-six Ozzfest shows in twenty-six cities across the United States had already sold out—and the concert wouldn't even kick off until July! Obviously, Ozzy's fans don't want to miss a chance to see the Prince of Darkness live! Fans in his homeland of the United Kingdom are just as dedicated. His upcoming concerts are already sold out, and they named him the Number 1 Rock Star 2003 in the United Kingdom, according to Virgin Radio. He is greeted with the same love and admiration in Sweden, Spain, and Japan. Anywhere that

The 2004 Ozzfest lineup poses for a group shot with Ozzy. Among the crowd are Rob Halford from the metal band Judas Priest (to Ozzy's right).

Kelly charms the media in London at the 2004 NME Awards. *NME* magazine is a popular British music monthly. Its readers choose each year's award winners.

Ozzy goes, he sells out concerts and finds fans who truly want to rock.

Rock 'n' Roll Princess

Kelly is also finding that she has dedicated fans. Several fan-sponsored Web sites have been created, and her concerts are well attended. In March 2004, Kelly released *Live at Electric Ballroom*, a DVD of one of her London concerts. The DVD showcases Kelly's energy as she performs twelve songs for a crowd of adoring fans.

Along with the fans, music critics have written about how much they love Kelly's sassy style and confidence. Many have said that her punky look and sound are a refreshing change amid all today's blond, ultra-thin female pop singers.

In 2004, Kelly also began working with a new team of producers and musicians for a punk-pop album scheduled to be released in late 2004. Kelly is also exploring acting and has been sought out to appear in television shows. She has also expressed an interest in playing Veruca Salt in a remake of the film *Willy Wonka and the Chocolate Factory.*

So despite a horrible accident, a crazy family, and their struggles with sobriety, Ozzy and Kelly are still going strong and show no signs of slowing down.

TIMELINE

1948	• December 3, John Michael "Ozzy" Osbourne is born.
1963	• Ozzy drops out of school at age fifteen.
1969	• Ozzy and some friends form the band Black Sabbath.
1970	• February, Black Sabbath debuts with self-titled first album; the groundbreaking album defines a new genre of music.
1971	• Ozzy marries Thelma Mayfair.
1979	• Ozzy leaves Black Sabbath; later he will reunite with Sabbath in 2000 to record new songs and to tour.
1981	• May, Ozzy bites the heads off two doves during a meeting with CBS Records; Ozzy divorces Thelma Mayfair
1982	• January, Ozzy bites the head off of a bat during a concert in Iowa.
	• July, Ozzy marries his manager, Sharon Arden.
1983	• September, Aimee Osbourne is born.
1984	• October, Kelly Lee Osbourne is born.
1985	• November, Jack Osbourne is born.
1993	• February, Ozzy wins a Grammy Award for Best Metal Performance for "I Don't Want to Change the World."
1996	• July, Ozzy and Sharon kick off Ozzfest.
2000	• February, Ozzy wins a Grammy for Best Metal Performance for "Iron Man."
2002	• March, *The Osbournes* reality television show debuts on MTV and quickly becomes the highest-rated original show in the station's history.
	• April, Kelly records the Madonna song "Papa Don't Preach."
	• June, the book *The Osbourne Family Album* is released.
	• July, Sharon Osbourne is diagnosed with colon cancer.
	• November, Kelly releases her first album, *Shut Up*.
2003	• April, Sharon is declared cancer-free.
	• September, Kelly releases her second album, *Changes*; Ozzy and Kelly begin touring the United Kingdom together.
	• December, Ozzy is critically injured in an ATV accident.
2004	• April, Kelly's parents confront her about her drug abuse and check her into a drug rehabilitation clinic; third season of *The Osbournes* debuts.

DISCOGRAPHY

Black Sabbath (Featuring Ozzy Osbourne)

1970	• *Black Sabbath* and *Paranoid*
1971	• *Master of Reality*
1972	• *Black Sabbath Vol. 4*
1975	• *Sabotage* and *We Sold Our Soul for Rock and Roll* (greatest hits)
1978	• *Never Say Die!*
1986	• *Greatest Hits*
1998	• *Reunion* (live)
2002	• *Past Lives* and *Symptom of the Universe* (compilation)

Ozzy Osbourne Solo

1980	• *Blizzard of Ozz* and *Diary of a Madman*
1982	• *Speak of the Devil*
1983	• *Bark at the Moon*
1986	• *The Ultimate Sin*
1987	• *Tribute* (live)
1988	• *No Rest for the Wicked*
1990	• *Ten Commandments* (greatest hits)
1990	• *Just Say Ozzy* (live) and *No More Tears*
1993	• *Live and Loud* (live)
1997	• *The Ozzman Cometh* (greatest hits)
1998	• *The Ozzfest* (live compilation)
2002	• *Live at Budokan* and *The Essential Ozzy Osbourne*

Kelly Osbourne

	• *Shut Up*
2002	• *Changes*
2003	

GLOSSARY

drug abuse Heavy use of illegal drugs such as marijuana and cocaine; unauthorized, heavy use of prescription drugs.

drug rehabilitation A program that helps people who are addicted to drugs or alcohol.

dyslexia A learning disability involving difficulties acquiring and processing language.

genre A category of art, such as paintings, music or literature, that is characterized by a certain style.

hallucinations A false perception with no basis in reality; a common symptom of severe mental disorder.

headbanger A musician or fan of hard rock or heavy metal.

heavy metal Fast-tempo music with a hard beat and electric guitars.

ominous Threatening or menacing; suggesting evil.

overtone A suggestion; an implied meaning.

profanity Vulgar language; also called cuss words, swear words, or four-letter words.

rabies A viral disease that attacks the immune system; transmitted through the bite of warm-blooded animals.

smitten Captivated; in love with.

Web Sites

Due to the changing nature of Internet links, the Rosen Publishing Group, Inc., has developed an online list of Web sites related to the subject of this book. This site is updated regularly. Please use this link to access the list.

http://www.rosenlinks.com/fafa/ooko

FOR FURTHER READING

Books

Clerk, Carol. *Diary of a Madman: Ozzy Osbourne: The Stories Behind the Songs.* New York: Thunder's Mouth Press, 2002.

Katz, David, and Michael Robin. *The Osbournes.* Kansas City: Roundtable Press, Inc., 2002.

Osbourne, Ozzy, and Harry Shaw. *Ozzy Talking: Ozzy Osbourne in His Own Words.* New York: Music Sales Corporation, 2002.

Osbourne, Ozzy, and Sharon Osbourne, et al. *Ordinary People: Our Story.* New York: MTV Books/Pocket Books, 2003.

DVDs

The Osbournes, The First Season, Miramax Home Entertainment, 2002.

The Osbournes, The Second Season, Miramax Home Entertainment, 2002.

The Osbournes, The 2-1/2 Season, Miramax Home Entertainment, 2004.

BIBLIOGRAPHY

ABC News. "Close Call for Ozzy. Osbourne Gives First Interview After Near-Fatal Accident." February 19, 2004. Retrieved February 23, 2004 (http://more.abcnews.go.com/sections/primetime/goodmorningamerica/ozzy_osbourne_040219.html).

CNN. "Ozzy Timeline: Bat Man to Family Man." April 12, 2002. Retrieved January 12, 2004 (http://www.cnn.com/2002/SHOWBIZ/TV/04/12/ozzy.timeline/index.html).

Katz, David, and Michael Robin. *The Osbournes*. Kansas City: Roundtable Press, 2002.

MTV. "Elton John Advises Kelly and Ozzy on Changing 'Changes.'" October 6, 2003. Retrieved April 3, 2004 (http://www.mtv.com/news/articles/1479560/20031006/story.jhtml).

MTV. "Kelly Osbourne Checks into Rehab for Painkiller Addiction." April 2, 2004. Retrieved April 3, 2004 (http://www.mtv.com/news/articles/1486155/20040402/story.jhtml).

Osbourne, Ozzy, and Sharon Osbourne, et al. *Ordinary People: Our Story*. New York: MTV Books/Pocket Books, 2003.

Ozzy.com. "Ozzy Update." January 1, 2004. Retrieved January 12, 2004 (http://www.ozzy.com/frameset.html).

INDEX

A

Arden, Don, 15

B

Beatles, 10-11, 14
Black Sabbath, 33–34
    drugs and, 33–34
    image of, 14
    influence of, 15
    Ozzy's departure
        from, 16, 34
    popularity of, 14–15
    sound of, 14, 15
    start of, 12, 14
Black Sabbath, 15
Black Sabbath Vol. 4, 31
Blizzard of Ozz, 18
Butler, Terrance
    "Geezer," 12

C

Changes (album), 26
"Changes" (song), 5, 6,
    29–31

D

Diary of a Madman, 18

H

heavy metal, 15

I

Iommi, Tony, 12, 14

J

John, Elton, 31

M

Mayfair, Thelma, 16, 18
MTV, 5, 6–7, 21–22

O

Ordinary People, 15,
    21, 33
Osbourne, Aimee, 11
Osbourne, Jack, 11,
    36–37
Osbourne, Jessica
    Starshine, 16
Osbourne, Kelly
    hair colors of, 36
    music career, 23–26,
        29–31, 40
    substance abuse and,
        33, 36, 37, 39
    tattoos of, 23, 27
Osbourne, Louis, 16
Osbourne, Ozzy
    ATV accident and,
        5–7, 31, 39
    in Black Sabbath, 12,
        14–15, 16, 33
    childhood of, 9–11
    dove/bat incidents
        and, 16–17,
        18, 22
    drug/alcohol abuse
        and, 16, 17,
        33–35, 36
    first marriage of,
        16, 18
    marriage to Sharon,
        18, 19, 35

solo career, 16, 18–19
    start in music, 11–12
    tattoos of, 23, 26
Osbourne, Sharon, 19,
    23, 26, 34, 37
    cancer and, 36
    marriage to Ozzy,
        18, 35
    Ozzfest and, 19
    as Ozzy's manager,
        16–17, 18
Osbournes, The (tv show),
    5, 21-23, 25, 30, 35,
    36, 37
Ozzfest, 19, 39

P

Paranoid, 15

S

Shut Up, 26

W

Ward, Bill, 12
Warner Brothers, 15

47

About the Author

Linda Saucerman is a writer and editor living in Queens, New York with her husband, Matt. Although she is not musically inclined, she has performed Ozzy's "Crazy Train" karaoke style.

Photo Credits

Cover (left) © Nina Prommer/Globe Photos Inc.; cover (right), p. 40 © Dave Hogan/Getty Images; pp. 1 (left), 30, 37 © AP/Wide World Photos; p. 1 (right) © Gareth Davies/Getty Images; pp. 4–5, 24 © Kevin Winter/Getty Images; p. 6 © Gareth Cattermole/Getty Images; pp. 8–9, 13, 17, 19, 22 © Neal Preston/Corbis; p. 20–21 © Reuters/Corbis; p. 25 © Steve Sands/New York Newswire/Corbis; p. 27 © Frank Trapper/Corbis; p. 28–29 © Getty Images; p. 32–33 © Barclay Graham/Corbis; p. 34 © Giulio Marcocchi/Getty Images; p. 38–39 © VaughYoutz/Zuma/Corbis.

Designer: Nelson Sá; **Editor:** Charles Hofer;
Photo Researcher: Nelson Sá